The Two Great Wars

Library of Congress Cataloging-in-Publication Data

Scott, Janine.
  The Two great wars / by Janine Scott.
      p. cm. -- (Shockwave)
  Includes index.
  ISBN-10: 0-531-17756-4 (lib. bdg.)
  ISBN-13: 978-0-531-17756-3 (lib. bdg.)
  ISBN-10: 0-531-15491-2 (pbk.)
  ISBN-13: 978-0-531-15491-5 (pbk.)
1. World War, 1914-1918. 2. World War, 1939-1945. 3. History,
Modern--20th century. I. Title. II. Series.

  D521.S43 2007
  940.3--dc22

2007016314

Published in 2008 by Children's Press, an imprint of Scholastic Inc.,
557 Broadway, New York, New York 10012
www.scholastic.com

08 09 10 11 12 13 14 15 16 17
10 9 8 7 6 5 4 3 2 1

Printed in China through Colorcraft Ltd., Hong Kong

Author: Janine Scott
Educational Consultant: Ian Morrison
Editor: Janine Scott
Designer: Matthew Alexander
Photo Researchers: Janine Scott and Nadja Embacher

Photographs by: Getty Images (army recruiting queue, p. 11; British Mark IV tank, p. 17;
Dunkirk rescue, p. 23); **Jennifer and Brian Lupton** (pro and con teenagers, pp. 32–33);
Photolibrary (Battle of Stalingrad, p. 27); **Stock X.chng** (p. 34); **Tranz/Corbis** (cover;
pp. 3–9; assassination of Archduke Ferdinand, p. 11; pp. 13–14; nurses at work in the
trenches, p. 15; p. 16; torpedo room, p. 17; pp. 18–21; London residents, milkman, p. 23;
pp. 24–26; underground resistance fighters, p. 27; pp. 29–31; Vietnamese child soldiers,
pp. 32–33); **Tranz/Popperfoto** (soldier using periscope, p. 15)

All illustrations and other photographs © Weldon Owen Education Inc.

SHOCKWAVE
SOCIAL STUDIES

The Two Great Wars

JANINE SCOTT

children's press®

An imprint of Scholastic Inc.

NEW YORK • TORONTO • LONDON • AUCKLAND • SYDNEY
MEXICO CITY • NEW DELHI • HONG KONG
DANBURY, CONNECTICUT

CHECK THESE OUT!

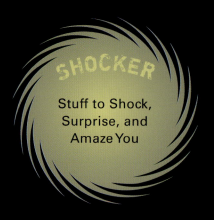

SHOCKER

Stuff to Shock, Surprise, and Amaze You

Quick Recaps and Notable Notes

Word Stunners and Other Oddities

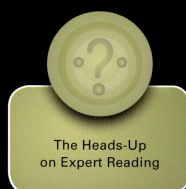

The Heads-Up on Expert Reading

Links to More Information

CONTENTS

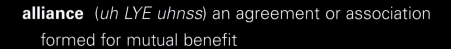

alliance (*uh LYE uhnss*) an agreement or association formed for mutual benefit

Allies (*AL eyes*) in World War I and World War II, the countries that fought on the side of Britain

armistice (*ARM iss tiss*) an agreement to stop fighting

Axis (*AK siss*) in World War II, the countries that fought on the side of Germany

Central Powers in World War I, the countries that fought on the side of Germany

front line the area between enemy territories where the fighting takes place

treaty a formal agreement to do with peace or trade between two or more countries

trench a long, narrow ditch dug by troops to provide protection from enemy fire

For additional vocabulary, see Glossary on page 34.

The word *trench* comes from the French *trenche*, meaning "a slice or ditch." So *trench warfare* took place in ditches, and a *trench coat* is a type of weatherproof garment made popular by British officers during World War I.

French soldiers in a **trench**, 1916

During the twentieth century, there were two world wars. When the first war began in 1914, most people thought it would last only a few months. But World War I – the Great War – lasted for four years. About nine million troops died. Twenty-one million more were wounded, and about six million **civilians** died – most of these from famine or disease. In fact, the Great War was not great at all. Although the **Allies** won, people on both sides suffered greatly. For the next ten years, people tried to recover from this terrible conflict.

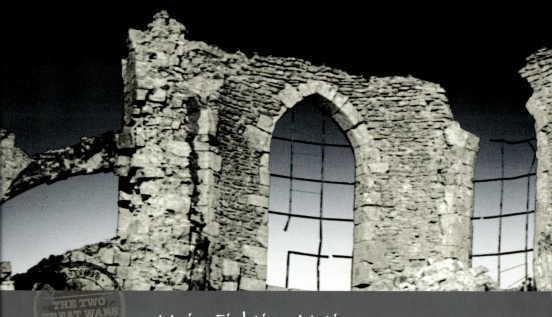

Main Fighting Nations

	Allies	Central Powers / Axis
World War I (1914–1918)	Allies: Great Britain, France, Russia (until 1917), Serbia, Italy (from 1915), Canada, Australia, Japan, New Zealand, South Africa, India, U.S.A. (from 1917)	**Central Powers**: Germany, Austria-Hungary, Ottoman Empire, Bulgaria (from 1915)
World War II (1939–1945)	Allies: Great Britain, France, Russia (from 1941), Canada, Australia, New Zealand, South Africa, India, China, U.S.A. (from 1941)	**Axis**: Germany, Italy (from 1940), Hungary (from 1941), Japan (from 1941)

In 1929, another disaster struck. The stock market crashed and the world economy collapsed. Japan and many European countries looked to strong leaders to solve their problems. Many leaders adopted policies of military expansion. World War II began just over 20 years after the end of World War I. This war took place not just in Europe but also in Asia and the Pacific. It cost the lives of about 60 million people. Of these, 17 million were military casualties. The other 43 million were civilians.

American soldier near Verdun, France, 1918

Battle Areas

| Europe (mostly Belgium, France, Austria-Hungary), Russia, Italy, Ottoman Empire, Palestine, Syria, Africa |
| Europe, Middle East, North Africa, Asia, Atlantic Ocean, Pacific Ocean and Islands |

Weapons and Defense

| Machine guns, **artillery**, rifles, poisonous gas, grenades, airplanes, tanks, ships, submarines, trenches |
| Tanks, bomber and fighter airplanes, artillery, machine guns, rifles, grenades, submarines, **radar**, atomic bombs, battleships, aircraft carriers, rockets |

The Deadly Ride

In the early 1900s, an extreme form of patriotism, called nationalism, swept across Europe. This caused a great deal of tension and hostility among many countries, as they competed for power and control. They wanted to gain territory within Europe, as well as in **colonies** in Asia and Africa. The colonies often provided them with raw materials for industry. This political tension led many countries to build up their military force. This, in turn, meant that the countries formed **alliances** with other countries for protection. Often these were done in secret.

On June 28, 1914, Archduke Franz Ferdinand and his wife were on a state visit to Sarajevo in Bosnia. The archduke was heir to the throne of Austria-Hungary. This powerful empire had controlled neighboring Bosnia since 1908. Bosnia's neighbor, Serbia, didn't like this. It wanted control of Bosnia. As the archduke and his wife traveled to the town hall, a Bosnian named Gavrilo Princip leapt out of the crowd, onto their car, and shot the archduke and his wife. Princip was linked to a Serbian terrorist group.

On July 28, Austria-Hungary declared war on Serbia. This also led to war with other countries. Germany and Austria-Hungary had an alliance. Russia, France, and Britain had their own alliance. Germany declared war against Russia on August 1 and against France two days later. Other nations declared war too. The Great War of 1914 had begun.

World War I Alliances

- Allies
- Central Powers
- Neutral countries

In 1914, there were five great powers in Europe: Britain, France, Russia, Germany, and Austria-Hungary.

Alliances

From the late 1800s, nationalism spread in many European countries. Countries formed alliances with other powerful countries. Countries also changed alliances.

1879: Germany and Austria-Hungary form an alliance as protection against a Russian attack.

1881: Russia, Germany, and Austria-Hungary form an alliance. They agree to remain **neutral** if any of them went to war.

1882: Italy, Germany, and Austria-Hungary form an alliance.

1894: Russia forms an alliance with France, deserting Germany and Austria-Hungary.

1907: Britain, Russia, and France form an alliance.

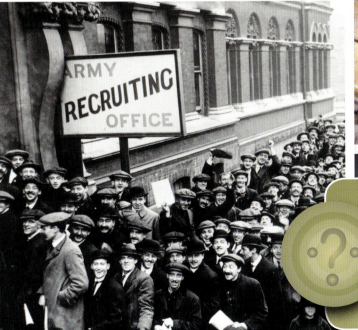

Men eager to become soldiers, England, 1915

As I was reading these pages, I found myself continually looking at the map. I find it really helps to use all the available information on the page.

The Fighting Fronts

Germany's war plan had been drawn up since 1905. Germany had the strongest army in Europe. However, it was in a difficult position. It had an enemy on either side: France on its western border and Russia on its eastern border. Germany's war plan involved invading and defeating France before attacking Russia. For the plan to work, Germany had to act fast, before Russia could organize troops.

On August 4, 1914, Germany sent more than a million soldiers into Belgium. They quickly advanced into northern France. By late November, a number of bloody battles had taken place. The Allies and the Central Powers suffered great losses. With the onset of winter, a **deadlock** occurred. Armies on both sides decided to defend their positions, rather than advance. They dug in, building **trenches** as protection against enemy fire. A 450-mile line of trenches stretched all along the Western Front, from the English Channel to the Swiss border. Often the enemy trenches were only a few feet away from each other.

World War I Battlefronts

Germany used trains to get troops to the battlefields quickly.
It built 13 railroad lines to transport soldiers to the French border.
The French rushed 6,000 soldiers to the battle in 600 taxis!

Major Battle Casualties

Marne, France: 1914	Verdun, France: 1916	Somme, France: 1916
British 12,733	British not involved	British 400,000
French 250,000	French 315,000	French 200,000
German 250,000	German 280,000	German 600,000

German troops, 1914

On September 6, the First Battle of the Marne played a key role in stopping Germany's swift defeat of France. Instead of sticking to the war plan, the Germans went east of Paris, near the Marne River. The original war plan had been to sweep west around Paris. In the battle, the Allies managed to halt the German advance.

Germany

Strengths
- alliance with Austria-Hungary
- strongest army in Europe
- a well-thought-out war plan

Weaknesses
- strong enemies on each side
- didn't stick to war plan

Stench of the Trenches

Trench warfare remained in a deadlock for about three and a half years. The smell of the trenches was overpowering, as dead bodies lay decaying. Soldiers in the trenches were also faced with rats, lice, rain, snow, and mud. There were periods of intense fear and fighting. There were also long periods of boredom. Most of the fighting took place at night. During the day, soldiers cleaned their rifles, repaired the trenches, wrote letters home, and played cards. The trenches were often makeshift and cramped. They were about six feet deep and six feet wide. There was often only enough room for two people to move along them. Soldiers who didn't keep their heads down could be killed by enemy fire. Trenches were usually fortified with sandbags and barbed wire.

Soldiers were often ordered to attack the enemy. They had to scramble up a ladder and leave the trenches. This was known as going "over the top." They ran toward an area known as "no man's land." On both sides, **infantry** were issued with rifles with fixed **bayonets**. However, they were usually gunned down by the enemy's machine-gun fire before they had a chance to use their bayonets. They stood little chance against a weapon that released 600 bullets a minute.

The origin of the word *bayonet* is unclear. Many people, however, think it comes from the French city Bayonne, where bayonets were first made.

SHOCKER

The rats in the trenches were known as corpse rats. They ate the decaying bodies and dead horses. Soldiers had contests to see who could catch the most rats.

German soldiers with captured rats

Periscope
Bayonet
Rifle

Did You Know?

The trenches were often filled with water because of rain, snow, and poor drainage. Many soldiers suffered from trench foot, which was caused by having constantly wet feet. The symptoms were red, swollen, and painful feet. Lice also spread a highly contagious disease called trench fever.

It was dangerous to raise your head above the trench **parapet**. Soldiers used camouflaged **periscopes** to check on enemy positions.

Trenches on Both Sides

Communication trenches

No man's land

Front-line trench

Reserve trench

Support trench

Both sides built a network of trenches. The fighting took place in no man's land and in front-line trenches. Behind these were support and reserve trenches, where soldiers rested before returning to the fighting on the **front line**. Supplies and soldiers moved between the front and rear along the many communication trenches. Soldiers and nurses carried the wounded on stretchers to the rear of the trench network.

British nurses help a wounded soldier in a trench onto a stretcher, 1915

Weapons of War

In 1914, both sides fought with rifles, bayonets, grenades, machine guns, and field artillery. The British had about eight machine guns per brigade, which consisted of about 4,000 soldiers. The casualties on both sides were enormous. In 1914, airplanes were still a recent invention. Both sides put the airplane to good use. Planes became spies in the sky. They took aerial photographs to show where troops, artillery, and trenches were located. Early warplanes didn't carry weapons, but the pilots often carried pistols. Before long, the role of airplanes changed. Fighter pilots soon took part in deadly **dogfights**.

On September 15, 1916, the tank rolled into battle for the first time. This British invention could travel over muddy ground, smash through barbed-wire barriers, and travel over trenches. Foot soldiers could also hide behind a tank as it advanced.

Another deadly weapon existed in World War I. It was poisonous gas. Both sides feared gas attacks. In 1915, during the Second Battle of Ypres (*EE pruh*), the Germans were the first to use this weapon. Soldiers were issued gas masks that covered their eyes, nose, and mouth. Soldiers in the trenches would rattle cans to let others know of a gas attack.

German soldiers and dogs with gas masks, 1916

SHOCKER

During the war, more than one million soldiers were gassed. About 91,000 died from the gas attacks. Many were blinded. Mustard gas burned the skin, lungs, and eyes. Soldiers and even their horses and dogs wore gas masks for protection.

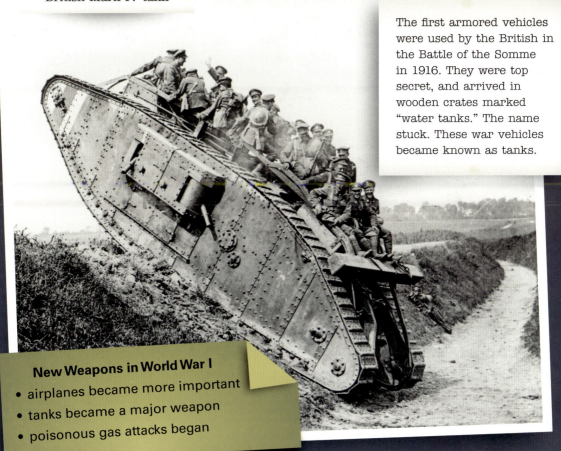
British Mark IV tank

The first armored vehicles were used by the British in the Battle of the Somme in 1916. They were top secret, and arrived in wooden crates marked "water tanks." The name stuck. These war vehicles became known as tanks.

New Weapons in World War I

- airplanes became more important
- tanks became a major weapon
- poisonous gas attacks began

Did You Know?

Fighter pilots earned the name *ace* if they shot down five or more enemy planes. The top ace of World War I from either side was German Baron Manfred von Richthofen. He was also known as the Red Baron because his plane was painted red. He shot down 80 enemy planes.

Torpedo room in German U-boat

German submarines, called U-boats, attacked British merchant ships. They hoped to cut off Britain's supplies, and starve the British into surrendering. By 1917, Britain had only six weeks' worth of supply of food and other supplies. Merchant ships started to travel in convoys. Destroyers escorted and protected them, firing **depth charges** at U-boats. The number of U-boat sinkings increased. The tactic worked. Britain didn't surrender.

1917–1918

Two major events took place during 1917. The United States entered the war on April 6. This was after German U-boats had sunk some U.S. cargo ships and a ship carrying U.S. civilians. The Great War became known as World War I because it involved countries from all around the world.

The other major event of 1917 was the Russian Revolution. The Russian people revolted against their country's leaders. They were tired of the severe food and fuel shortages and the great human losses of the war. The emperor, Czar Nicholas II, was forced to give up his throne on March 15, 1917. Then another revolution occurred in October. **Communist** leader Vladimir Lenin took control of the new government. He brought an end to the fighting on the Eastern Front. On March 3, 1918, he had signed a peace **treaty** with Germany.

Now the Germans thought that they would win the war. They shifted troops to the Western Front. They wanted to move quickly before the United States had time to move troops to Europe. However, with one million U.S. servicemen fighting in Europe by August 1918, those hopes were soon dashed. The Germans asked for peace when they realized they could not win. At the eleventh hour of the eleventh day of the eleventh month of 1918, an **armistice** between Germany and the Allies was signed. The war was finally over. The countries that fought in the war had lost most of a generation of young men.

In war, the Allies fought against the Central Powers. In death, enemies were often buried close to one another in makeshift graves.

SHOCKER

In World War I, more soldiers died from flu and other diseases than from battle wounds.

Just five days before Armistice Day, this elderly French couple knew the war was nearly over. It would bring an end to four years of German occupation. Here they thank two American soldiers.

The red poppy is a symbol of the poppies that grew in the fields of Flanders, Belgium, where fierce fighting took place. Many people wear poppies on Veterans Day, which is on November 11. This day celebrates the armistice that ended World War I on November 11, 1918. It also honors those who died fighting in all wars.

Allied soldiers and French civilians celebrate the armistice.

Peace Turns to War

By 1918, World War I had ended, but the tensions in Europe were far from over. Towns and cities lay in ruins. People were hungry and homeless. Many Germans resented the peace treaty signed in Paris on June 28, 1919. The Treaty of Versailles made Germany accept the blame for the start of World War I. The Allies made the Central Powers surrender their weapons. Germany was not allowed tanks, airplanes, submarines, or artillery. It was made to pay war damages. It was expected to take Germany 70 years to pay the total amount. The Allies also drew up new European borders. Germany lost land to France, Denmark, Poland, Belgium, and Czechoslovakia. It also lost it colonies.

Then, in 1929, the **Great Depression** hit Europe. It created even more economic hardship. Many people lost their jobs, money, and homes. One person who resented the hardships and the way Germany was treated after the war was Adolf Hitler. In the 1920s, he became the leader of the German Workers' Party, which later became known as the Nazi Party. In March 1933, the Nazi Party took total control of Germany. That same year, Hitler made himself a **dictator**. He used terror and the secret police, known as the Gestapo (*guh STAH poh*) to maintain his power. The Gestapo imprisoned and executed any person who opposed the government. Hitler refused to obey the Treaty of Versailles. He stopped Germany's war payments. He put many things, such as newspapers and radio, under Nazi control. He outlawed all other political parties.

German machine guns handed in for scrap, 1920

Did You Know?

During the 1920s and 1930s, dictators rose to power in three other powerful countries:
Italy: Benito Mussolini
Soviet Union: Joseph Stalin
Spain: General Francisco Franco

Unemployment was high when Hitler came to power. He put people to work on projects, such as building a highway system. Hitler actually planned to use the highways to transport tanks and troops through Germany quickly. Unemployed people also built tanks, ships, submarines, and warplanes. Hitler was rearming Germany and preparing for war.

Hitler prepared German children for war too. All children who were ten or older had to join organizations that promoted Nazi beliefs. All boys fourteen years of age or older joined the Hitler Youth. They were taught military skills and took part in physical fitness exercises. German girls fourteen or older joined the Society of German Maidens.

From 1933, German Jews began to lose all their rights. Hitler believed that light-skinned, blue-eyed, and blond Germans, or Aryans, were a superior race. He blamed Germany's problems on non-Aryan people, such as Jews. On November 9, 1938, Hitler and the Nazi Party's hatred of Jewish people was shown in an event called the Night of Broken Glass. Nazi supporters smashed Jewish-owned storefronts and looted the businesses. They burned down nearly all of Germany's **synagogues**.

The Lightning War

Adolf Hitler wanted to conquer Europe. On September 1, 1939, Germany invaded Poland and started the lightning war, or *Blitzkrieg*. This German war tactic relied on speed. More than 1.25 million German troops swept into Poland. Great Britain and France declared war on Germany two days later. Then, on September 17, 1939, Russia invaded Poland's eastern border. Germany and Russia had secretly become allies. In the first half of 1940, Germany went on to invade and occupy

Denmark, Norway, Belgium, the Netherlands, Luxembourg, and northern France. Hitler then set his sights on crossing the narrow English Channel and invading Britain. With France's surrender, Britain now stood alone in its battle against the German advance. Early on in the war, the United States had declared itself neutral.

Hitler assumed that Britain would now surrender. However, he underestimated the British people and their leader. Winston Churchill became the British prime minister on May 10, 1940. Churchill's "never surrender" speech was made on June 4, 1940. He called for Britain to defeat Nazi Germany, whatever the cost.

To conquer Britain, Hitler first had to conquer Britain's Royal Air Force (RAF). The Battle of Britain started in July 1940. Both sides wanted control of the air. German fighter planes bombed factories, airfields, and ports in England and Scotland. In September, they started bombing London. The air raids became known as the Blitz. Despite having fewer aircraft than the Germans, the RAF fought back with great courage. In May 1941, Germany accepted defeat in the Battle of Britain. Hitler called off the invasion of Britain.

In late May 1940, 338,000 Allied troops found themselves trapped on the beaches of Dunkirk in northern France. Britain launched a brave and daring rescue. Every seaworthy British ship and boat, from large destroyers to small pleasure craft, crossed the English Channel to evacuate the troops. Most of the troops were evacuated under enemy fire over the course of one week.

Churchill's Words

"… we shall go on to the end … we shall fight in the seas and oceans … we shall defend our island, whatever the cost may be … we shall fight on the beaches, we shall fight on the landing-grounds, we shall fight in the fields and in the streets, we shall fight in the hills; we shall never surrender …"

One of the things that Hitler didn't count on was the fighting spirit of the Londoners during the Blitz. Even during the worst bombing periods, they carried on with daily life as an act of defiance.

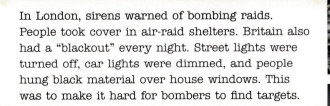

In London, sirens warned of bombing raids. People took cover in air-raid shelters. Britain also had a "blackout" every night. Street lights were turned off, car lights were dimmed, and people hung black material over house windows. This was to make it hard for bombers to find targets.

Allies Become Enemies

With the failure to win the air battle, Hitler now turned his sights to Russia. At the start of the war, Germany and Russia were allies. However, on June 22, 1941, Hitler turned on his ally. He had only befriended Russia to ensure that Russia didn't fight against Germany. Germany now intended to control Russia. German troops advanced quickly into Russia. They looked set for victory. However, luckily for Russia and the Allies, the weather played an important role in preventing a German victory. In October, heavy rains fell. German tanks and artillery got stuck in mud, slowing their advance. Then, in early December, a severe winter began. The Germans were not prepared. Their equipment broke down. They had inadequate winter clothing. Many soldiers suffered from frostbite and hunger. Russia's leader, Joseph Stalin, now allied Russia with Britain.

In the same month, two powerful nations, the United States and Japan, joined the war. The United States declared war on Japan on December 8, 1941, a day after Japan bombed U.S. warships and planes in Pearl Harbor, Hawaii. This surprise attack finally drew neutral United States into the war.

Italy was on Germany's side. However, by late 1941, Hitler was beginning to think that Italy was more a hindrance than a help. Hitler had to send German troops to Greece and northern Africa to help Italian troops. This delayed Hitler's invasion of Russia by a month. This loss of time would prove disastrous. German troops not only had to battle Russia's large Red Army, it also had to battle the bitter Russian winter. Russian soldiers were more adequately dressed in warm, snow-colored clothes and lined boots.

Russian soldiers

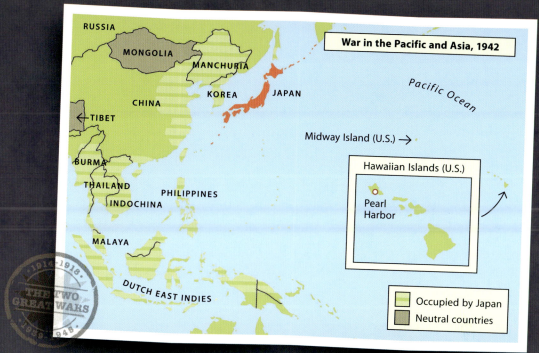

War in the Pacific and Asia, 1942

RUSSIA
MONGOLIA
MANCHURIA
KOREA
JAPAN
CHINA
←TIBET
BURMA
THAILAND
INDOCHINA
PHILIPPINES
MALAYA
DUTCH EAST INDIES

Pacific Ocean

Midway Island (U.S.) →

Hawaiian Islands (U.S.)
Pearl Harbor

Occupied by Japan
Neutral countries

The Rise of Japan

Like many leaders at this time, Emperor Hirohito of Japan sought expanded territory and more natural resources for industry. Japan signed a pact with Germany and Italy in 1936. In 1937, Japan attacked China. In 1940, it invaded Indochina. Tensions grew between Japan and the United States, Great Britain, and the Netherlands. These countries stopped selling oil and other natural resources to Japan. Japan responded by expanding its war in the Pacific region. This included plans for a surprise attack on a U.S. naval base on Pearl Harbor, Hawaii. This drew the United States into the war.

The Japanese attacked Pearl Harbor with 350 airplanes. Twenty-one American ships and about 300 American planes were destroyed or damaged in the early-morning attack.

Main Events of 1941

- Germany loses Battle of Britain
- Germany invades Russia
- Russia becomes ally of Britain
- Japan bombs Pearl Harbor
- Japan and United States enter the war

Fighting On

The war was fought in the air, at sea, and on land. Many battles and many millions of lives were lost, including those of innocent civilians. The Jews and other minorities in German-occupied countries faced danger and death. Most were rounded up and transported to ghettos or **concentration camps** in Poland and Germany. Millions were **exterminated** in gas chambers. Many of the prisoners were shot, worked or starved to death, or died of disease. In 1942, the Nazis implemented their plan called the "final solution." They built death camps in Eastern Europe, where they gassed to death millions of Jews.

In 1942 and 1943, battles raged across Europe. In 1942, the battle for Stalingrad in Russia was a turning point of the war in Europe. More than a million Russian soldiers died defending the city. However, they won this important battle. They stopped the German advance into Eastern Europe. In 1942, the Allies also won key battles in North Africa. The Allies invaded Sicily on July 10, 1943. On September 3, 1943, Italy surrendered **unconditionally** to the Allies.

In Warsaw, Poland, the Nazis forced Jews to live in an area of the city that became known as the Warsaw Ghetto. As many as 500,000 Jews lived in the ghetto at one point. However, disease, hunger, executions, and deportations to concentration camps greatly reduced the number. In April 1943, thousands of Jews revolted against the Germans. As punishment, the 60,000 Jews who remained in the Ghetto were killed or sent to the concentration camps.

The word *ghetto* comes from a seventeenth-century Italian word, meaning "part of a city where Jews are restricted." Later, *ghetto* was used as a term for any minority group in a crowded urban area.

RUSSIA

Stalingrad

GERMANY

Some of the bloodiest hand-to-hand fighting of World War II took place during the Battle of Stalingrad. Finally, on January 31, 1943, the Germans surrendered. They had lost the Battle of Stalingrad.

From 1940, France was a German-occupied country. Many French people joined an **underground** resistance movement that worked to defeat the Germans. They published newspapers, sent information to the Allies, and helped Allied soldiers escape. They also attacked German forces. There were resistance movements in Belgium, Poland, and Holland.

Midway

In June 1942, the Japanese navy planned a second surprise attack on the U.S. naval base at Midway, a tiny island in the Pacific Ocean. This time, however, the plan was discovered by U.S. communications intelligence. The U.S. fleet was waiting in ambush. Although both navies lost ships in the battle, the outcome was a big win for the U.S. It was the most important naval battle of the war. After Midway, the U.S. was able to take the offensive in the Pacific.

D-Day

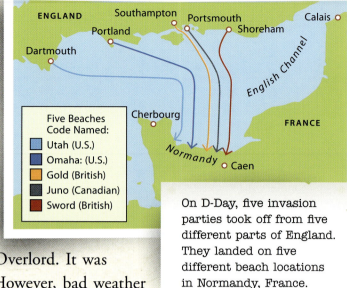

Five Beaches
Code Named:
- ◼ Utah (U.S.)
- ◼ Omaha: (U.S.)
- ◼ Gold (British)
- ◼ Juno (Canadian)
- ◼ Sword (British)

On D-Day, five invasion parties took off from five different parts of England. They landed on five different beach locations in Normandy, France.

In 1942, the Allies began planning a large-scale invasion of northern France. The plan was to liberate France and the rest of German-occupied Europe. The invasion's code name was Operation Overlord. It was planned for June 5, 1944. However, bad weather and rough seas delayed the attack until June 6.

Five beaches in Normandy were chosen as the invasion landing sites. The Allies took the Germans by surprise. The German leaders had expected the Allies to cross at the narrowest part of the English Channel to the French seaport of Calais. However, the Allies used 2,700 ships to transport 176,000 soldiers to Normandy. By 6:30 A.M., soldiers stormed along the 60-mile stretch of beaches. Fierce fighting took place. Many of the Allies were gunned down by machine-gun fire before they even made it off the boats or onto the beaches. However, the landings were a success. All five beaches were secured by the Allies at the end of the first day.

Some Allies headed west to capture the port of Cherbourg. Other Allies headed east toward Caen. The advance inland was slow. The Allies' aim was to push toward Paris, then through Belgium toward Germany. Hitler, sensing defeat, ordered his generals to burn Paris. However, his generals disobeyed the order. On August 25, 1944, the Allies entered Paris and liberated the city. They hoped that the war would end in 1944. It soon became clear that it wouldn't. Hitler ordered a surprise attack in Belgium and Luxembourg. It was a last, desperate attempt to prevent Germany from losing the war. The battle in the Ardennes Forest began on December 16, 1944. It was the largest battle fought by the Americans in World War II.

The Germans thought that the Allies would invade France, so they laid mines in the water and along the beaches. They also fortified the beaches with obstacles.

Paratroopers invaded Normandy early in the morning on June 6. Planes and gliders dropped them behind enemy lines. Their aim was to capture important railroads and bridges.

Did You Know?

Photographer Robert Capa took the first photographs of D-Day. Three rolls were quickly sent to London to be processed. However, a mistake was made in the darkroom. Only eight photos survived.

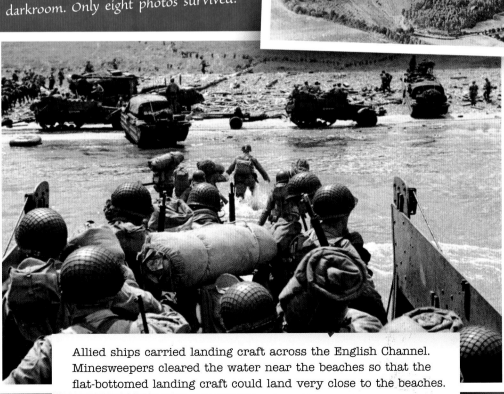

Allied ships carried landing craft across the English Channel. Minesweepers cleared the water near the beaches so that the flat-bottomed landing craft could land very close to the beaches.

Liberation, Jubilation!

In early 1945, a victory for the Allies in Europe was inevitable. As the Russians marched toward the German capital of Berlin, Hitler hid in a reinforced underground shelter in the city. He ordered Germany to continue to fight. However, many of his officers refused to carry on. Many German soldiers surrendered. Hitler and his wife, Eva Braun, committed suicide on April 30, 1945. By May 7, the Germans had surrendered unconditionally. After nearly six years of fighting, the Allies had won the war in Europe!

The Allies liberated cities throughout Europe. They came across many war **atrocities**. When they liberated the concentration camps, they were shocked to see the prisoners. Some were too weak to stand. Many had diseases, such as **typhus**. Many lay dead in large open pits. Some inmates were found locked inside the camps – the guards had fled to avoid capture.

Many towns and cities rejoiced when they saw the Allies. They had long awaited liberation. Throughout Europe and in the United States, people danced in the streets and went to V-E (Victory in Europe) Day parades. However, this was victory only in Europe. The war in the Pacific against Japan still raged on. It was September 2, 1945 before there was finally worldwide peace.

On April 29, 1945, prisoners in the concentration camp in Dachau, Germany, celebrated their liberation by American soldiers. The day before liberation, most German soldiers had abandoned the camp.

I've seen programs about atomic bombs and concentration camps. So I already know something about this topic. That makes reading about it easier.

Hiroshima, 1945

1914-1918 · THE TWO GREAT WAR

Liberation came at a heavy price. On July 26, 1945, the Allies ordered Japan to surrender unconditionally, or face being destroyed. Japan didn't surrender. So on August 6, the first atomic bomb was dropped on Hiroshima. On August 9, a second atomic bomb was dropped on Nagasaki. Japan signed a surrender agreement on September 2, 1945. This day became V-J (Victory over Japan) Day.

Japan Surrenders

By 1944, the U.S. was advancing island by island toward the home islands of Japan. The U.S. had superior resources in terms of pilots, planes, and ships. Japan was determined to fight to the end for its emperor. One weapon Japan used was the kamikaze pilot. These were suicide pilots who attacked enemy ships by diving directly into them. Almost 4,000 pilots lost their lives on these missions.

New York City, May 7, 1945

SHOCKER

About 100,000 people died in Hiroshima. In Nagasaki, 40,000 people lost their lives. The heat from the bombs was so intense that it melted metal. Skin often hung loose from people's bodies.

31

During World War I, many men volunteered to join the military. They were patriotic and wanted to fight for their country. Later in the war, men older than eighteen were called up, or **conscripted**. Many young boys were also eager to go to war. They saw it as an exciting way to see the world. Most had no idea about the horrors that lay ahead. Even though many of them were not yet eighteen, their parents granted them permission to join up.

WHAT DO YOU THINK?

Should children under eighteen be allowed to fight in a war if they want to?

PRO

I think that many children around the world who are under eighteen are already earning a living, have left home, or have families of their own. They are making their own decisions about their own lives. They should have the right to choose to fight.

Some who didn't get permission forged their birth certificates and lied to the authorities about their age. Soldiers had to be eighteen to fight. However, many soldiers were as young as fourteen. Today, child soldiers are still fighting in wars around the world. In January 2000, the United Nations ruled that children under age eighteen should not take direct part in conflict. However, this hasn't stopped children being used as soldiers in war.

CON

I think that children should be protected from the realities of war. Sometimes they might be forced against their will to take part in war. Since the United Nations made these rules, it should make sure that they are enforced.

GLOSSARY

Artillery

artillery (*ar TIL uh ree*) a large gun used on land

atrocity an extremely cruel act

bayonet (*BAY uh net*) a kind of blade attached to a rifle, used for fighting

civilian (*si VIL yuhn*) a person not in the armed services

colony (*KOL uh nee*) a settlement under the rule of a parent country

communist a person or government that believes in organizing a country so that all the land, houses, and factories belong to the government or community, and the profits are shared by all

concentration camp a camp where people are imprisoned or killed for their race or beliefs, especially in Nazi Germany during World War II

conscript (*con SKRIPT*) to order to join the military

deadlock a situation in which no progress is made

depth charge an explosive charge designed to explode under the water at a certain depth

dictator a person who has complete control of a country, often ruling it unjustly

dogfight a close combat between two enemy airplanes

exterminate to kill living things to the point of wiping them all out

Great Depression the worldwide collapse of business in the 1930s

infantry (*IN fuhn tree*) the part of the army that fights on foot

neutral (*NOO truhl*) impartial or unbiased

parapet (*PAR uh puht*) a protective wall or earth defense along the top of a military trench

paratrooper a soldier who is equipped to be dropped by parachute from an airplane

periscope (*PEHR uh skohp*) an instrument that consists of a long tube with a reflecting mirror at each end, through which a person can see something that is out of sight

radar (*RAY dar*) a device that locates objects by reflecting radio waves off them and receiving the reflected waves

synagogue (*SIH nuh gog*) a building in which Jewish people worship

typhus (*TY fuhss*) an infectious disease that causes headaches, fever, and delirium

unconditionally completely and absolutely, with no conditions or limitations

underground secret

FIND OUT MORE

BOOKS

Adams, Simon. *World War I*. DK Eyewitness, 2004.

Corrigan, Jim. *Causes of World War II*. OTTN Publishing, 2005.

Freedman, Russell. *Children of the Great Depression*. Clarion Books, 2005.

Tanaka, Shelley. *D-Day: They Fought to Free Europe From Hitler's Tyranny*. Hyperion, 2004.

Zeman, Anne and Kelly, Kate. *Everything You Need to Know About American History*. Scholastic Reference, 2005.

Ziff, John. *Causes of World War I*. OTTN Publishing, 2005.

WEB SITES

Go to the Web sites below to learn more about the World Wars.

www.digitalhistory.uh.edu/modules/ww1

www.digitalhistory.uh.edu/modules/ww2

www.bbc.co.uk/schools/worldwarone

www.ushmm.org/outreach/nrule.htm

http://library.thinkquest.org/5711

INDEX

ABOUT THE AUTHOR

Janine Scott loves writing both fiction and nonfiction books for children of all ages. She especially enjoyed writing this book, because World Wars I and II have been a particular interest of hers for many years. Most of the events of the two great wars were not great at all. There were enormous military and civilian losses and suffering. However, Janine says that, among the horrors of war, there are many uplifting stories about spies, great escapes, cracking secret codes, and human kindness. Janine hopes that this book will spark readers' interest in this fascinating subject and inspire them to investigate further the complicated human and military events of these large-scale conflicts.